ANALYZING ENVIRONMENTAL CHANGE

ANALYZING
OIL PRODUCTION
AND CONSUMPTION

ASKING QUESTIONS, EVALUATING EVIDENCE, AND DESIGNING SOLUTIONS

PHILIP STEELE

Cavendish
Square

New York

Published in 2019 by Cavendish Square
Publishing, LLC, 243 5th Avenue, Suite 136,
New York, NY 10016

Copyright © 2017 Wayland, a division of
Hachette Children's Group

First Edition

Cataloging-in-Publication Data

Names: Steele, Philip.
Title: Analyzing oil production and
consumption: asking questions, evaluating
evidence, and designing solutions / Philip
Steele.
Description: New York : Cavendish Square,
2019. | Series: Analyzing environmental
change | Includes glossary and index.
Identifiers: ISBN 9781502639356 (library
bound) | ISBN 9781502639363 (pbk.) | ISBN
9781502639370 (ebook)
Subjects: LCSH: Petroleum industry and
trade--Juvenile literature. | Petroleum--
Juvenile literature. | Energy consumption--
Juvenile literature.
Classification: LCC HD9565.S834 2019 | DDC
338.2'7282--dc23

Produced for Cavendish Square by
Tall Tree Ltd
Editors: Jon Richards
Designers: Ed Simkins

Printed in the United States of America

CONTENTS

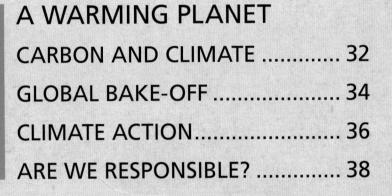

IT'S TIME TO TALK ABOUT
OIL AND GAS

We fill up the car with gas and off we drive. This simple act would have amazed our ancestors, but to us it seems completely normal. We live in an age in which petroleum and natural gas have given us freedom of movement and a comfortable life.

POWER SOURCE

Refineries process oil and gas so that we can power our cars, trains, ships and aircraft. We use these amazing fuels to heat our homes, to run our power stations, to make all kinds of plastics and chemicals. They have made our lives so much easier. What's not to like?

Oil pumps, also called 'nodding donkeys,' bring crude oil up from deep beneath the surface. These pumps are in China. Crude oil is then refined into different fuels.

DO WE HAVE A PROBLEM?

Scientists are saying that gases from factories and exhaust from cars are overheating our planet and changing the climate. So is it wise to keep filling up the car? Can we even break that habit if we want to? Is there enough oil to go around, and will it keep flowing forever? Is it the future of energy or is the Oil Age already coming to an end? Is it being overtaken by smarter and cleaner technologies?

OIL RIGS

Some oil sources lie buried beneath the seabed. Offshore oil rigs extract this oil. There are more than 1,400 oil rigs in the world. Some employ up to 200 workers. Occasionally rigs spill oil, which damages marine life.

FARM FUEL

We use oil and petroleum in almost every part of our everyday lives - from heating our homes to harvesting the food we eat.

SMOG

This polluted street is in northeast China. Pollutants from power plants, factories and vehicles can create a dangerous soup of chemicals that can choke the atmosphere in cities, damaging the lungs and airways of inhabitants.

We have never been so dependent on oil, but it could be causing more damage than ever. In each chapter of this book we'll look at different aspects of the topic of oil and gas, exploring and discussing the issues involved. There are vital questions to be raised and discussed.

Let's talk about them.

5

WHAT ARE OIL AND GAS?

Oil and natural gas are hydrocarbons – they are made up of carbon and hydrogen atoms. Oil as it comes out of the ground is called crude. The liquid is often sticky and black, or sometimes it has a reddish-brown color, and may be light or heavy, depending on how easily it flows. Natural gas taken from the ground is made up of a mixture of hydrocarbons, mostly methane (CH_4).

NUMBER CRUNCH

The typical mix in crude oil is about 85 percent carbon, 13 percent hydrogen and 2 percent impurities, such as sulphur.

impurities

carbon

hydrogen

NUMBER CRUNCH

Natural gas is composed of 95 percent methane, 3.2 percent ethane and small amounts of other components.

3.2% ethane

95% methane

FOSSIL FUELS

Oil and gas are organic substances. They were formed from living matter between 10 million and 600 million years ago. That is why we sometimes call them fossil fuels. Countless small plants and animals living in the sea died and were covered by mud. Over the ages, movements in Earth's crust squeezed and squashed the mud to form rock. The rocks slipped, tilted up or folded over. The hydrocarbons either soaked into the more porous rocks, or were trapped in pockets between hard rocks.

OIL IN HISTORY

In a few places, hydrocarbons seeped to the surface of the ground. For thousands of years people used these for lighting or sometimes for making weapons, such as flaming arrows. Sometimes, people dug wells to access underground oil.

Until the nineteenth century, the Chinese used oil pipes made of bamboo. In 1859, in the USA, Edwin Drake was the first to use machinery – a steam-powered rig – in order to drill for oil. The Oil Age had begun.

A flame burns off excess gas from a drilling rig far out in the Gulf of Mexico.

SO MANY USES

Just why are oil and gas so important? Because they affect almost every aspect of our lives. We don't only refine and process them for use as fuels. We use them as a starting point for thousands of other industrial applications. Whenever we walk into a bathroom, a kitchen, a school, an office, a factory, a supermarket, a garage or a gym, we are surrounded by oil-based products.

ASPHALT
Workers lay asphalt on the surface of a motorway.

DETERGENTS
Cleaning products are made from petrochemicals.

AIR MILES
Jet airliners can use a huge amount of fuel. A Boeing 747 Jumbo jet will burn through 5 gallons (19 L) of fuel every mile (1.6 km) it flies.

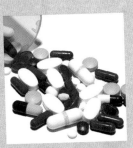

MEDICINE
Petroleum is used to make many medicines.

PLASTIC
A huge variety of products, like these water bottles, are made from plastic.

FUEL FRENZY

Petrol or diesel is used to power cars, trucks, trains and ships. The roads we drive on are surfaced with asphalt. Aviation fuel ('avgas') is used in many aircraft, while jet fuel is made of kerosene, sometimes blended with naphtha, which both derive from oil and gas. In the home, central heating boilers are fired by oil or gas. In many power stations, it is oil or gas that makes it possible for us to generate electricity.

FABRICS
Some fabrics, such as lycra and nylon, contain petrochemicals.

Since petroleum is so widely used, changes in its price can affect more goods than you may realize. It is a key ingredient in everything from footwear to food.

COSMETICS
Mineral oil and petroleum are the basic ingredients in many cosmetic products.

FOOD
Petroleum-based food preservatives are often found in fast foods. Food packaging is often made from polystyrene and other plastic materials.

LUBRICANTS
Motor oil, which is derived from petroleum, provides lubrication for the millions of cars around the world.

PLASTICS AND CHEMICALS

Petrochemicals are used to make dyes, cleaning fluids, pesticides, fertilizers and medications. Plastics take many forms – from bags, packaging and toys, to parts of fridges, dishwashers, phones, computers and building materials. Even artificial hips and knee joints can be made of plastic.

Oil and its products are everywhere on the planet. How are these substances used? How do they react with the natural environment and with human health? These are some of the biggest questions facing us today.

NUMBER CRUNCH

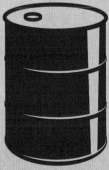

Oil is measured by barrels. One barrel is equal to 42 gallons (159 L). In 2016, the world was consuming about 96 million barrels every day.

FROM ROCK TO PUMP

Oil raises big questions from the moment it is discovered to the moment it reaches the gas pump. Firstly, there are practical and technical questions. Are the rock formations suitable, on land and offshore? Can the oil be accessed easily by drilling? Is there enough oil and will it make money? Are operations safe for the workers on the job?

HIGH IMPACT

There are wider questions, too. How will local communities be affected? What kind of impact will drilling and production have on the environment? Will operations pollute land, sea and air? Will the product itself make climate change even worse?

WORKING THE RIG

Workers known as roughnecks handle the shaft of the drill bit at an oil well in Colorado, USA. They are overseen by a foreman known as a tool pusher.

SKILLS AND SAFETY

Geologists search for new reserves of oil using smart satellite technology and seismometers. Test drilling is followed by the real thing. Engineers design massive offshore platforms, fixed or floating. Across an oil field, there may be many wells and hubs with pipes laid between them. Workers who are flown out to the rigs by helicopter grapple with drill bits, concrete casing for the borehole, and with the pressure valves that prevent a blowout. Safety procedures are strict.

Platform supply vessels pump water onto the blazing wreck of the *Deepwater Horizon* oil rig, while the US coastguard searches for the missing crew.

CATASTROPHE

But it can all go wrong. In 2010 the *Deepwater Horizon* rig in the Gulf of Mexico suffered a wellhead blowout and exploded into a fireball. Eleven crew members were killed. The rig sank and a sea floor oil gusher flowed for 87 days before finally being capped. The spill of crude oil into the ocean was disastrous for tourism, fisheries, coasts and wildlife. It was the largest accidental oil spill in the history of the industry.

LET'S DISCUSS...
NEW OIL RESERVES

• are easier to locate and access than ever before.

• create job opportunities.

• drive new technologies.

• put the environment at risk during drilling and production.

• may be at the center of a major disaster.

• may disrupt local communities and their way of life.

FLARES
AND FRACKERS

Often natural gas and oil come from the same wells. If the gas contains pockets of oil (known as 'slugs'), they are removed after the gas has been piped to the terminal. If it's the gas that isn't wanted, it may be burnt off as a flare or, as flares pollute the air, the unused gas may be injected back into the underground hydrocarbon reservoir.

SHALE GAS

Natural gas can also be extracted by a process called hydraulic fracturing, or fracking, a terma now widely used in the United States. This can take place on land or offshore. Shale rock that contains gas is drilled and then injected with water, chemicals and sand at high pressure. This breaks up the rock and forces out the gas.

Shale gas production has given a boost to the US economy and reduced prices. Its supporters say that it is safe and clean, if properly controlled.

But fracking has many critics. They say fracking wastes huge amounts of water and pollutes the water table (the level of water under the ground). They say the break up of shale rock can cause subsidence and earth tremors. This would be particularly dangerous in built-up areas.

A shale gas drilling rig mines a bore hole in a field in Colorado. Fracking wells provide 43 percent of the oil in the United States, and 67 percent of the gas.

> "... Fracking will accelerate climate change, pollute our environment and lock us into yet more dependence on fossil fuels at precisely the time when we need to be moving in the opposite direction."
>
> Caroline Lucas, English Member of Parliament for the Green Party, 2014

Oil sands are generally a mixture of clay, sand and water that contains bitumen. This hydrocarbon is thick and gooey, like tar. In Canada it is being accessed by injecting the ground with steam and chemicals or by partial burning. Opponents warn of severe pollution and environmental damage. They say contaminants from oil sands leak into rivers and degrade the Canadian Arctic, one of the world's remaining wild places.

STICKYSTUFF

A worker handles a clump of oil sands. Removing the usable oil from this can be expensive and complicated.

CONTROVERSIAL MINING

Huge machinery is needed to scoop enormous amounts of oil sands out of the earth. This oil sands mine is in Alberta, Canada.

LET'S DISCUSS... FRACKING

- accesses gas that other methods can't reach.
- brings down the price of gas.
- helps the economy.

- pollutes the water table.
- may cause subsidence and earth tremors.
- wastes water on a large scale.

1 SHIFTING THE PRODUCT

EXTRACTING OIL AND GAS

Once hydrocarbons are out of the ground, they need to be stored or prepared for use. Crude oil is processed at a refinery where impurities such as sulphur must be removed. The oil is then heated to a temperature of 748°F (398°C). Cooling the oil to different temperatures produces gasoline, diesel, kerosene, and so on. Crude oil and product oil may need to be carried long distances. Natural gas can also be transported, by pressurizing it into liquid form.

PIPE IT!

Pipelines are a very convenient way to move hydrocarbons. The pipes can be made of plastic or steel sections, and laid under the sea, underground or overground. Pumps keep the liquid flowing along between about 3 and 7.5 miles per hour (5–12 km/h).

There can be problems. Pipelines may cause environmental damage, particularly in fragile habitats such as the deep-frozen Arctic tundra. Pipelines can cross several countries, and are easily turned off during political or economic disputes. They risk being attacked by armed forces or terrorists.

A gas pipeline zigzags its way across the tundra landscape of western Siberia in Russia. The world's longest gas pipe runs between Russia and Ukraine.

14

TANKERS AND SPILLS

Moving oil by sea is the job of supertankers, some of which can carry 3 million barrels of crude. Smaller tankers are needed to access smaller ports and many canals. Oil tankers are also at risk of attack. In 2009, the MV *Sirius Star*, carrying oil worth $100 million, was captured by Somali pirates. They collected a ransom of $3 million.

In the past, oil spills from both pipelines and tankers have caused terrible pollution on land and sea. In recent years, the record has improved, but even so, 2015 saw two major spills as a result of tanker collisions, in Singapore and in Turkey.

OIL SPILL
Oil released from a damaged tanker floats on the surface of the water and covers the rocks and sand of any coastline it is washed up against.

KILLING WILDLIFE
Oil from a spill harms wildlife. Sea birds lose the waterproof nature of their feathers, meaning that they cannot swim and so drown.

NUMBER CRUNCH
The world's biggest ever supertanker (1979-2009) was the *Seawise Giant*. It had a length of 1,503 feet (458 m). That's longer than four football fields.

LET'S DISCUSS...
OIL SUPERTANKERS

- can carry huge cargoes.
- are the most cost-effective way of moving oil.
- can be used just for storage of oil if required.

- may be too large for some ports and canals.
- may spill oil as a result of collision or shipwreck.
- can be attacked or hijacked even by small vessels.

POLAR DRILLING

Drilling for oil is difficult. In the Arctic Ocean it would present a unique challenge. The region around the North Pole is frozen all year round. Outer regions melt during the brief summer.

QUESTION IT!
SHOULD WE DRILL IN THE ARCTIC?

MOST OF THE RESERVES LIE beneath water, at depths of about 1,640 feet (500 m). It's doable. After all, Americans have been drilling in Alaska's Prudhoe Bay oil field since 1968.

THE ARCTIC OCEAN has been losing ice in recent years. In the future, it will be easier to get oil and gas from this region.

THE ARCTIC IS THOUGHT TO CONTAIN ABOUT 30 PERCENT of the world's unknown reserves of gas and perhaps 13 percent of all the unknown oil, estimated to be about 160 billion barrels. There is money to be made.

Even though they are harsh places, the Arctic tundra and polar ecosystems are very fragile.

THE REASON THE ARCTIC OCEAN IS LOSING ICE is because of climate change. By moving in to drill for even more oil, humans would only be making things far, far worse.

CAN YOU IMAGINE A MAJOR OIL SPILL IN THE ARCTIC? The Arctic ecology depends on its rich marine life, its fishes, seabirds, walruses, seals and polar bears.

ARCTIC PEOPLES LIVING IN THE FAR NORTH depend on a clean environment for their livelihood.

IN A REMOTE AREA, it would be very hard to move in all the people and equipment needed to clean up a spill. After all, the winters are long, dark and bitterly cold.

"Caribou migrating in the Arctic are for me one of the ultimate wild spectacles... To witness it is to feel the divine. It is not easy to feel the divine in the oil fields."

R. Glendon Brunk, US environmentalist, *Yearning Wild*, 2001

TRAFFIC JAM!

Human beings have a love affair with oil. It began with the invention of the gasoline-fueled motor car in 1886. The internal combustion engine still fascinates us today. The combustion of fuel mixed with oxygen releases gases at high pressure. The engine kicks into action – we have movement and power.

Traffic jams clog many of the roads leading into major towns and cities, leading to hours of frustration for drivers and high levels of pollution.

FOUL FUMES

Unfortunately, we also have the exhaust, a mixture of gases created by the burning of the fuel. These may be treated in a catalytic converter to make them less toxic. Even so, the gases that do pour out of the exhaust pipe pollute the air. They include carbon dioxide, nitrogen, water vapor and small traces of other chemicals.

THE RISK TO HEALTH

Exhaust fumes may kill about 5,000 people a year in the United Kingdom alone. They have been linked to illnesses such as asthma, heart disease and lung cancer. Car exhaust may mix with other forms of air pollution and react with sunlight, creating a horrible, choking smog in big cities such as Beijing and Los Angeles.

WHAT CAN BE DONE?

We can keep traffic out of our city centers. We can walk or bike to school or work. We can carpool or use public transportation. Car makers can also improve their fuel efficiency and emissions testing, or research other fuels and car designs.

TESTING CARS

In many countries, cars are regularly inspected to check that they are still safe to drive and that their engines do not produce too many pollutants.

LET'S DISCUSS... CARS WITH GAS ENGINES

- give us freedom of movement.
- support an important industry.
- are cleaner that they used to be.

- block our cities with traffic jams.
- pollute the air with exhaust fumes.
- contribute to climate change.

NUMBERCRUNCH

In 1960 the US registered 75 million cars and light trucks. In 2015 it registered 258 million.

2 THE POWER GENERATORS

Electricity powers the world. But many of the power stations that generate that electricity are themselves powered by fossil fuels. Oil, gas and coal are all used to heat water to create steam. This drives the spinning turbines that generate electricity. The burning of these hydrocarbons releases gases into the atmosphere, polluting the air we breathe and bringing on climate change (see pages 32–33).

COAL POWER

Steam rises from the cooling towers of a coal-fired power station in Germany. Germany is rapidly expanding its renewable energy sources and hopes to rely far less on stations like this one.

POWER STATION POLLUTION

Coal is the dirtiest of all the fossil fuels because it creates the most pollution when it is burned. Gas is the cleanest option. But all release carbon dioxide. Fossil fuels may also release sulphur dioxide (SO_2). This may mix with water vapor in the atmosphere and fall as acid rain, harming forests, lakes, wildlife and even buildings. We can reduce harmful emissions from power stations, for example by installing filters in chimneys, but producing energy in this way is never completely clean. Add in mining, drilling, transport and construction, and it's clear—generating power with hydrocarbons is no way to tackle pollution.

ENERGY TRANSITION

Germany has already turned away from generating power with hydrocarbons and nuclear fuels. Both are finite; they eventually run out. Both carry environmental risk. Both may depend on insecure supplies from overseas. Germany is concentrating instead on developing renewable technologies such as wind and solar power.

This wind farm is located in northern Germany, near the North Sea. Germany has nearly 28,000 wind turbines and plans to build many more.

Coal - 23%

Gas - 30%

NUMBER CRUNCH

In 2015, 23 percent of UK electricity was generated by coal, 30 percent by gas, 24 percent by renewable sources such as solar and wind, 21 percent by nuclear, and 2 percent from oil and other sources.

THINK ABOUT... FOSSIL FUELS

- pollute the air.
- contribute to climate change.
- are not renewable.

FANTASTIC PLASTIC?

We don't always make the connection between oil and plastics. But by way of the oil refinery and the production of naphtha, a vast range of plastic products has been produced since the 1950s. These line the shelves of the supermarket. They are wrapped in plastic, we carry them in plastic bags, we even pay for them with a plastic card.

THE WONDER MATERIAL

Polymers are chemical compounds. They are formed from long chains that repeat the same group of molecules. Thermoplastics, such as polystyrene, can be softened by heating or hardened by cooling. Thermosets, such as polyurethane, become stronger as they are heated. They are rigid and cannot be remolded. The things plastics can do are amazing. They can be bendy, stretchy, soft, hard, rigid or strong.

Because it is cheap to produce and can provide a tight, airtight seal, plastic is often used as a storage material for food and drink.

WASTE AND TRASH

Plastics have been so successful that we use them far too often. Unnecessary supermarket wrappings for foods fill our garbage cans. Flimsy plastic bags blow around city streets. Plastic waste pollutes the world's rivers. Tiny pieces of plastic collect in the oceans, where they are swallowed by fish and other animals. Some plastics are made to be biodegradable, breaking down naturally. Otherwise, the process can take 500 to 1,000 years. The US only recycles about 27 percent of its plastics. The rest is burned or ends up in a landfill.

A mound of plastic waste piles up on Thilafushi in the Maldives. This artificial island was created as a landfill. It is 4.3 miles (7 km) long and 0.12 miles (0.2 km) wide.

NUMBER CRUNCH
In the US, about 35 billion plastic water bottles are thrown away each year.

PLASTIC POISONS

Some plastics have added chemicals which can cause cancer or other health problems. Some release toxic chemicals if they are heated, crushed or become worn out.

LET'S DISCUSS...
PLASTICS

• provide all sorts of useful objects.

• are cheap to manufacture.

• can sometimes be recycled.

• are often used wastefully.

• may contain harmful toxins.

• pollute the world's oceans.

23

2 CHANGING THE PLANET

Few technologies are all good or all bad. Few of them have changed our lives as much as oil and gas. They have made human dreams a reality, allowing us even to fly around the world. But in doing so, have they damaged our planet and ruined our way of life?

IT COULD BE SAID that hydrocarbons created the modern world and shrunk it. The transport revolution opened up the world to travel, trade and understanding of other cultures.

FOSSIL FUELS have driven economic growth, creating jobs and allowing poor countries to develop.

POWER STATIONS FIRED by fossil fuels have brought us light, heat and hot water. These have made it easier for us to study, to keep clean and healthy, to cook meals, to work in factories and offices.

FOSSIL FUELS have allowed us to develop new technologies and completely new materials, such as plastics.

QUESTION IT!
HAS OIL CHANGED OUR WORLD FOR THE BETTER?

THE WORLD MAY HAVE BECOME easier to travel, but this has often led to a destruction of local cultures and unfair trade.

OIL HAS MADE SOME PEOPLE, companies and countries very rich, but has left many others poor. It has not brought peace or equality to all.

FOSSIL FUELS have polluted land, sea and air. They have filled the world with plastic trash. They have destroyed habitats and wildlife. They have created health problems.

Old cars lie rusting in Death Valley, California. During the 20th century, an abundance of cheap oil made motor cars affordable for millions of people.

THE MOST SERIOUS CASE against oil and gas? Climate change. It's happening now and oil and gas make it worse.

25

BLACK GOLD

For thousands of years, gold has been valued as the ultimate symbol of wealth. Since the 1900s, it has had a less sparkly rival – crude oil. Oil has made a few individuals unbelievably rich. John D. Rockefeller (1839–1937), founder of the Standard Oil Company, made a personal fortune worth more than $340 billion in today's money.

OIL RICH OR OIL POOR?

Access to oil makes countries rich or poor. In the deserts of Arabia and the Persian Gulf, poor fishing villages have been transformed into cities with palaces and skyscrapers, thanks to oil. Some countries, such as Venezuela, depend on exporting oil and gas to run their national economy. Other countries, such as Japan, have no oil and gas and have to import most of their energy needs.

This Ferrari supercar is parked on the street in Dubai. Wealth from oil production has made many places in the Middle East some of the richest in the world.

> "Some people find oil, some don't."
> J. Paul Getty (1892–1976), US oil billionaire

UPS AND DOWNS

The Organization of the Petroleum Exporting Countries (OPEC) tries to manage the world market in oil, but the business has very big ups and downs. Prices may be decided by supply and demand, by forecasts of new discoveries or technologies, by the risk of war or of economic troubles, or by competition from shale gas in the United States. Oil prices affect the transport costs of all goods and how much those goods cost. They affect the cost of living as a whole, as well as the prices we pay at the gas pump.

OIL MAGNATE
John D. Rockefeller (on the left) became the world's first billionaire through fortunes he made in oil, banking and real estate. He is pictured here with his son, John D. Rockefeller Jr., in 1915.

LET'S DISCUSS...
OIL WEALTH

- can help a country develop.
- boosts world trade.
- creates new jobs.

- can vanish overnight if the price falls.
- benefits the rich rather than the poor.
- makes oil companies too powerful.

27

3 POLITICS AND POWER

Oil and gas mean big money, and that means political power. Whether or not one country is sitting on the right kind of rocks for hydrocarbons may come down to history or to pure luck, a bit like winning the lottery. That has never stopped other countries trying to win control of that wealth, by means of politics or commerce, or even by war. China, for example, has claimed some remote islands hundreds of miles from the mainland as their own in order to have drilling rights.

ENERGY INDEPENDENCE

No nation wishes to depend on another for importing fuel. It puts them in a weak position. Western Europe fears its reliance on the gas pipeline from Russia, because that supply can be switched off. Energy independence allows political and economic independence. In a globalized economy, only renewable energy offers a really secure supply. No other country can turn off the wind or the sun.

Damaged oil wells burn in Kuwait following the retreat of the Iraqi army in 1991, sending pillars of black smoke into the sky.

WHO OWNS THE OIL?

The US, France and the UK have tried to rearrange the politics of the oil-rich Middle East for more than a hundred years. Western oil companies gained control of oil production in Persia (later Iran) in 1908. Democratically elected Iranian politicians who tried to nationalize the industry and control its prices were removed from power.

THE OIL WARS

Why do armies, guerrillas or terrorists go to war over oil? They may wish to protect or control transport routes, such as canals or pipelines. They may wish to gain control over profitable oil fields. They may wish to damage the oil wells of their enemy. Oil played a major part in World War I (1914–18), World War II (1939–45), the Suez Crisis (1956), the Biafran War (1967–70), and in most of the wars in the Middle East and North Africa from 1980 to the present day.

WORTH FIGHTING FOR?

In wartime, every effort is made to cut off an enemy's supply of fuel. Here, an American bomber attacks an oil refinery in Romania, an ally of Nazi Germany, during World War II.

NUMBER CRUNCH

In 1990, Iraqi forces retreating from Kuwait set fire to over 600 Kuwaiti oil wells.

LET'S DISCUSS...
OIL WARS

- cost millions of lives.
- damage the environment and the economy.
- rarely have any winners.

29

SERVING THE PUBLIC?

Who owns and accesses oil and gas reserves and in whose interest? There are many players. There are big oil corporations and their shareholders. There are national governments who award licenses for drilling and operating. There are state-owned companies. There are also powerful individuals, heads of state or politicians. Are they working just for themselves, or does society as a whole do well out of the deal?

QUESTION IT!
DOES THE OIL INDUSTRY SERVE THE PUBLIC INTEREST?

LOCAL AND INTERNATIONAL REGULATION of the oil industry can protect the environment and public health and safety.

THE OIL CORPORATIONS have the technical know-how and the money to develop new oil fields. Their operations provide employment and benefit the wider economy. The government might spend oil revenues from tax or state-owned reserves on education, healthcare or housing.

MANY OF THE WEALTHIEST oil millionaires in history have donated their own money to the arts, education and research, as have big corporations such as BP.

MANY OIL CORPORATIONS have economies that are larger than those of major nations. They include Royal Dutch Shell, Exxon Mobil, BP and PetroChina. Governments in democratic countries are more likely to be accountable to the public than are corporations.

The Greenpeace ship *Arctic Sunrise* has been used in a number of environmental protests against large corporations involved in oil, coal and whaling.

OIL CORPORATIONS SPEND many millions of dollars each year lobbying politicians and giving money to political campaigns.

PRO-OIL GOVERNMENTS may take extremely harsh action against opponents. In 1995 the writer Ken Saro-Wiwa, a champion for the rights of the Ogoni people living in the Niger Delta oil fields, was hanged. In 2013, 28 Greenpeace activists and two journalists were arrested at gunpoint and held in jail in Russia for six months after an Arctic drilling protest.

THE OIL INDUSTRY FUNDS campaigns to discredit and undermine environmental campaigners who oppose their operations.

4 CARBON AND CLIMATE

Carbon dioxide (CO_2) is part of the natural cycle of life on Earth. We breathe the gas out and plants take it in. The oceans and the forests all absorb large amounts of it. CO_2 is one of several gases in the atmosphere that keep the Earth's surface warm. These 'greenhouse gases' prevent some of the Sun's heat from escaping.

GLOBAL WARMING

In the last 150 years or so, the natural balance of gases in Earth's atmosphere has changed. CO_2 levels are now the highest they have been for three million years and the oceans are becoming more acidic. The greenhouse gases are trapping more and more warmth in the lower atmosphere. The planet is warming very rapidly.

Energy from the Sun is reflected by the atmosphere and by Earth's surface back out into space.

1

ATMOSPHERE

LET'S DISCUSS...
CARBON DIOXIDE

- supports plant life on Earth.
- helps make the planet warm enough to live on.
- is absorbed into the oceans.

- can be produced by burning oil or gas.
- is upsetting the balance of the atmosphere.
- helps to overheat the planet.

THE COST OF CHANGE

The Earth's climate is changing. That is nothing new. The planet has seen ice ages come and go, with warmer periods called interglacials in between. There have been smaller blips too, lasting just a hundred years or so. But nearly all scientists now agree that today's change in climate is being caused by the burning of hydrocarbons by humans, by emissions from traffic, power stations, and factories. Large areas of forest that used to take in CO_2 are being cut down and burnt to create space for agriculture. The CO_2 released into the atmosphere, along with other greenhouse gases such as methane (CH_4) and nitrous oxide (N_2O), are turning up the heat.

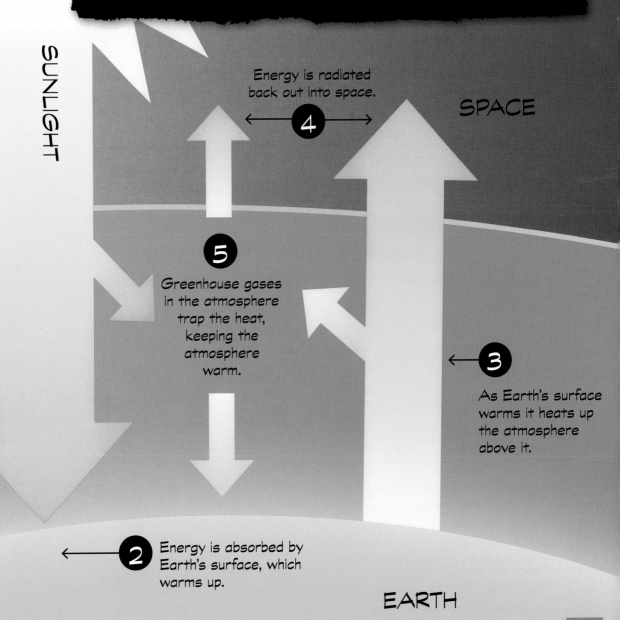

SUNLIGHT

Energy is radiated back out into space.

4

SPACE

5

Greenhouse gases in the atmosphere trap the heat, keeping the atmosphere warm.

3

As Earth's surface warms it heats up the atmosphere above it.

2 Energy is absorbed by Earth's surface, which warms up.

EARTH

GLOBAL BAKE-OFF

As the world warms, scientists collect data from around the world and from satellites in space. It is sometimes hard to tell which events are happening because of climate change, and which would be happening anyway because of local climate patterns. But gradually a bigger picture does emerge. Massive computer power is used to work out models for what might happen next.

Low-lying islands, such as Kiribati in the Pacific Ocean, could be lost completely to rising sea levels if climate change continues unchecked.

EXTREME WEATHER

Global warming will mean that some parts of the planet will become very hot indeed. There will be long droughts, more forest fires and more land will turn into desert. However other regions may receive more rain, because the warmer atmosphere can hold more water vapor. There will be more tropical storms, more floods and more uncertainty. Global warming will make the ocean expand, causing sea levels to rise. Melting ice in the Arctic and Antarctic will add to the flooding.

ACTION STATIONS

Humans will have to make tough decisions. Which land should they abandon and which should they defend with sea walls? Will people have to move? Will there be shortages of food and water? Already, we are faced with extreme weather events such as droughts. Perhaps the biggest question is about time: is there still time to deal with climate change, or are we doing too little, too late?

SEMI-DESERT

The Bardenas Reales in Spain is a natural semi-desert created by local weather patterns. It receives very little rain throughout the year. However, many more such semi-deserts may be created by climate change.

LET'S DISCUSS...
CLIMATE CHANGE

- is now recognised by almost all scientists.
- is already being tackled.
- may inspire new technologies and solutions.

- may be more severe than expected.
- is being denied by some politicians.
- cannot be halted quickly.

"Climate change is no longer some far-off problem; it is happening here, it is happening now."

Barack Obama, 44th President of the USA, 2015

CLIMATE ACTION

Scientists first raised questions about greenhouse gases and global warming back in 1896. In the 1960s, the rise in CO_2 levels was confirmed. In 1968, scientists warned the American Petroleum Institute that fossil fuels could damage the environment worldwide. The oil industry rejected those claims and funded campaigns to challenge the science. During the 1970s and '80s, there was growing public interest in the environment.

EARTH SUMMITS

By 1992, climate change had moved to the top of the agenda for the United Nations (UN). The United Nations Conference on Environment and Development (UNCED) was held in Rio de Janeiro, Brazil. This 'Earth Summit' was attended by over 100 governments, while 17,000 people came to a Global Forum organized by non-governmental organizations. In 1997, an agreement called the Kyoto Protocol was signed in Japan, committing countries to the fight against climate change.

In 2013, a crowd of up to 50,000 gathered in Washington, DC, to protest against the building of a pipeline carrying oil from Canada to the Gulf of Mexico.

SETTING TARGETS

A Paris UN conference in 2015 agreed to a limit of 3.6°F (2°C) above normal levels, while aiming for a 2.7°F (1.5°C) limit. The lower figure could mean zero CO_2 emissions at some point between 2030 and 2050. Many campaigners expressed doubt that these targets would be reached. The upper limit would still mean that huge problems lie ahead. Any increase above that would be disastrous. Even with zero emissions, the effects of climate change already under way could last for hundreds or even thousands of years.

PARIS PROTEST
While governments met at the UN conference in Paris, protesters gathered outside to make their feelings clear.

LET'S DISCUSS...

TEMPERATURE INCREASES

- of under 3.6°F (2°C): impact on polar ice, extreme weather events.
- of under 5.4°F (3°C): loss of coral reefs, water shortage, farming problems.
- of under 7.2°F (4°C): species extinctions, migration, food shortages.
- of under 9°F (5°C): massive flooding, starvation, and disease.

"We must now agree on a binding review mechanism under international law, so that this century can credibly be called a century of decarbonization."

Angela Merkel, Chancellor of Germany, 2015

ARE WE RESPONSIBLE?

There has been a heated public debate about climate change. It has raged for more than 25 years, and many people still think it's a hoax or some conspiracy. But we have to go with the evidence. Among scientists, the question is as good as settled. It's happening, and is chiefly caused by greenhouse gases.

A GROUP CALLED the Intergovernmental Panel on Climate Change (IPCC) was set up in 1988 by two United Nations agencies, the World Meteorological Organization and the UN Environment Programme.

THE IPCC STATES that there can be no doubt that climate change is taking place. Over the last century the planet warmed by 1.4°F (0.8°C) and the sea level rose by 4 to 8 inches (10–20 cm). It declared with 95 percent confidence that human activities have probably caused all global warming over the last 60 years. Most of the world's leading scientists agree.

QUESTION IT!
ARE HUMANS REALLY RESPONSIBLE FOR CLIMATE CHANGE?

THE IPCC does not carry out its own research. Its job is to study and compare scientific research from around the world and to draw its conclusions.

QUESTION: Doesn't the increase in sunspots over recent years give another, natural explanation for global warming?

A 2013 REVIEW of 4,014 scientific reports found that 97 percent agreed that global warming was taking place and that it was caused by humans.

ANSWER: No, evidence tells us that the Sun is actually cooling at the moment. The two things are not related.

QUESTION: Aren't there many completely natural climate cycles, such as the El Niño current in the Pacific Ocean?

ANSWER: True, El Niño has been affecting drought in southern Africa. Not all climate events are the result of global warming. Climate change is a complex interaction of many different factors.

5 CLEANER OPTIONS

A carbon footprint is a measurement by weight of the total amount of CO_2 used to support a particular activity. For example, it might refer to one person's vacation, factoring in the flight, the ride to the airport and so on. Measurements like these help us to see how each one of us can cut down on carbon.

SMALLER FOOTPRINT
As well as using less energy, people can reduce their carbon footprint by using renewable energy sources, such as solar power.

WHAT CAN BE DONE?

Governments, companies and law makers can look into various ways of dealing with the CO_2 problem.

• They can improve the environment. Protecting forests or planting new ones provide carbon sinks that absorb emissions.
• They can capture CO_2 from refineries or factory chimneys and store it in a carbon sink or underground reservoir.
• They can create zones in cities to avoid traffic jams, keep out high-emission vehicles and encourage cyclists and pedestrians.
• They can develop electric cars or non-fossil fuels such as hydrogen, biodiesel or alcohol.

• They can regulate existing power stations and invest in new zero-carbon renewable sources.
• They can cut down on waste from existing power grids and develop new smart grids and storage.
• They can increase taxes on fossil fuels.
• Under the Kyoto Protocol, nations can 'trade' in carbon quotas, swapping their liabilities. Critics say this carbon market is too complicated and fails to get to grips with the bigger problems that we face.

LET'S DISCUSS...
ELECTRIC CARS

• don't use fossil fuels.
• are cheaper to maintain.
• have good performance.

• need plenty of charging stations.
• have a limited range.
• cost a lot in electricity.

Many towns and cities now provide recharging stations for electric vehicles, such as this car.

41

OIL FREE?

With so many parts of our way of life dependent on oil and its products, can we really kick the habit of this fossil fuel? What would we use to replace it and do we have the desire and technology available to create an oil-free world?

HOW MANY MORE times will we send young people to kill other young people so we can fight wars for oil, gas and other resources?

IT CANNOT BE WORTH destroying the last, beautiful wildernesses on Earth, such as the Arctic, in order to produce fuels that are no longer essential.

THE RISKS OF CLIMATE CHANGE are too huge. We must break the hydrocarbon habit completely and use all our skills and knowledge to find out new and better ways of making things, traveling and generating power.

QUESTION IT!

SHOULD WE LEAVE OIL AND GAS IN THE GROUND?

The lights glow from an oil refinery where crude oil is changed into a wide range of products from tar to gasoline.

WHAT WILL OUR WORLD be like when we have filled the oceans with plastic, destroyed the coral reefs, polluted the rivers and lakes with oil and destroyed our birds and fishes?

WE FACE AN UNKNOWN FUTURE. We must develop all technologies but use our resources wisely. Oil and gas have many uses that do not contribute to climate change. We can obtain oil and gas without destroying the landscape.

43

THE FUTURE OF OIL AND GAS

For a long time people have been wondering just how much oil and gas is left in the ground. At some date, all the hydrocarbons that can be easily extracted will have been used up. However, it seems that as soon as anyone predicts that oil has passed its peak, more reserves are discovered, or new technologies are developed for accessing hard-to-reach hydrocarbons.

CLEANER AND MORE EFFICIENT

The oil and gas will likely be there, if we want them, for quite some time. They may be used for all sorts of jobs. New technologies will be needed to make them efficient, cleaner and safer. We need to cut not just fossil fuel emissions, but also the waste and the trash and the toxins in plastics.

The giant solar power plant is in Seville in Spain. An array of mirrors in a central tower concentrates sunlight and shines in at hundreds of solar panels.

RUNNING ON EMPTY?

But the world is already changing fast and fossil fuels are being replaced. Dirty technologies such as fracking or extracting oil from oil sands will be unnecessary. Electric cars are already with us. Solar, wind, tidal and wave power are being developed rapidly, and will need to be if we are to manage climate change. Maybe energy will be generated not in huge power stations, but within the materials we all use to build our homes or roads, which could act as solar cells and batteries.

MOTOR OIL
A routine car check usually involves checking the motor oil levels. Electric cars have no need for oil.

LET'S THINK ABOUT...
NEW DIRECTIONS

- may be able to end hydrocarbon pollution.
- can bring an end to wasting resources.
- include alternative technologies.

GLOSSARY

ASPHALT
A sticky, black, semi-solid form of petroleum used for surfacing roads, roofing and flooring.

BITUMEN
Also called asphalt (see above).

CARBON
A chemical element found in oil and natural gas as well as all living things.

CATALYTIC CONVERTER
A device fitted into the exhaust of a car that converts toxic gases into less harmful ones.

CLIMATE
The weather conditions in an area over a long period.

COMBUSTION
The process of burning something, like fuel mixed with oxygen in the internal combustion engine.

COMPOUND
A substance made of two of more separate elements, like hydrogen and oxygen.

CRUDE OIL
Oil in its natural, raw state, as found in the ground or oil well, before it is refined or processed.

DIESEL
A type of oil used as fuel in diesel engines.

ECOLOGY
The relationships between groups of living things and their surroundings.

EMISSIONS
The release of gases or pollutants into the atmosphere, particularly when fossil fuels are burned.

EXHAUST
A pipe in a car through which gases and fumes produced by the engine are expelled.

FERTILIZER
A substance added to soil to help plants grow.

FLARE
A brief burst of flame or light.

FOSSIL FUELS
Organic substances formed from living matter, like gas, coal and oil.

FRACKING
Shale rock that contains gas is drilled and then injected with water, chemicals and sand at high pressure. This breaks up the rock and forces out the gas.

GEOLOGIST
A person who studies rock, layers of soil and the physical properties of the Earth.

HYDROCARBONS
Oil and natural gas are hydrocarbons, a compound of hydrogen and carbon.

KEROSENE
A fuel made from distilling and heating oil and especially used in jet engines.

METHANE
A flammable, colorless gas that makes up 95 percent of natural gas.

MOLECULE
The smallest possible particle of a substance.

NAPHTHA
A flammable oil containing various hydrocarbons, made by distilling petroleum, shale or coal.

NATIONALIZE
When a national government takes ownership of or controls a certain industry, like the oil industry.

NATURAL GAS
A flammable gas, consisting largely of methane and other hydrocarbons, found in its natural state underground.

OIL SANDS
Loose sands that are saturated with a sticky form of petroleum, sometimes called tar. Found in extremely large quantities in Canada.

ORGANIC
Formed from natural, living substances, such as soil or crude oil.

PESTICIDE
A substance made up of petrochemicals that destroys insects and animals that harm plants and crops.

PETROCHEMICALS
Substances obtained from the distillation of petroleum or natural gas and used in a wide range of products, materials and plastics.

PETROLEUM
A type of flammable oil and liquid mixture of hydrocarbons obtained by oil wells.

PLASTICS
A material derived from petrochemicals that can be molded into solid objects. It is used in all sorts of products such as toys, computers, phones and building materials.

POLYSTYRENE
One of the most widely used plastics that can be softened when heated and hardened when cooled. It is commonly used as protective packaging or as disposable cutlery.

POLYURETHANE
A type of plastic that becomes hard when heated and is used to make various products, to include coatings for floors.

POROUS
A type of rock or other material that has small holes that allow liquid or air to pass through.

POWER STATION
A place where electrical power is generated for distribution.

RECYCLE
To make something new from something that has been made or used before.

REFINERY
A place where unwanted substances in something, such as in oil, are removed.

RESERVOIR
A place where something, often a large supply of water, is kept in store.

SEISMOMETERS
A device that measures the movement of the ground.

SHALE
A soft kind of rock formed from mud or clay that can be split easily.

SMOG
Fog or haze made worse by smoke or chemical pollutants in the atmosphere.

SOLAR POWER
Using the sun's rays especially to produce heat or electricity.

SUBSIDENCE
The gradual caving in or sinking of an area of land.

SULPHUR
A yellow chemical element that has a strong, unpleasant odor. It is removed from crude oil in a refinery.

TEST DRILLING
A procedure to determine the type and extent of reserves of oil underground.

THERMOPLASTIC
A plastic material that becomes soft when heated and hardens again when cooled.

THERMOSET
A plastic substance that sets permanently when heated and cannot be remolded.

TOXIC
Containing poisonous substances.

WATER TABLE
The highest underground level of rock or soil that is completely soaked with water.

INDEX

PICTURE CREDITS